BANNERS, RIBBONS & SCROLLS

An Archive for Artists and Designers
503 Copyright-Free Designs

Edited by
CAROL BELANGER GRAFTON

DOVER PUBLICATIONS, INC., NEW YORK

PUBLISHER'S NOTE

Banners, ribbons and scrolls are among the most useful elements in graphic design. Their derivation from curved, flexed or spiral arrangements of paper or cloth in three dimensions gives them a somewhat sculptural quality that can impart pomp and flair to any composition. As enclosures for type in headings, advertising and packaging, these devices highlight the message and add a touch of class.

The sources of the graphic material collected here are varied. Many were culled from late nineteenth-century periodicals, and so reflect the unabashed eclecticism of Victorian taste. The commercial artists of the period borrowed freely from past artistic traditions; Gothic, Renaissance, baroque, classical and even mock-Egyptian styles of ornament are all represented. Many examples of Art Nouveau design are included as well. Runs of the following periodicals provided the bulk of the material: *Cassell's Magazine, Century Magazine, Fliegende Blätter, Frank Leslie's Illustrated Newspaper, The Graphic, Illustrated London News, The Inland Printer, Scribner's Monthly* and *St. Nicholas.* Miscellaneous sources include various catalogues of stock cuts from engraving and type-founding houses; collections of bookplates; and early nineteenth-century copybooks of elaborate pen-flourish work.

Graphic designer Carol Belanger Grafton has selected and arranged the hundreds of banners, ribbons and scrolls in this treasury for ready use by advertisers, art directors, illustrators, découpeurs and other artists and craftspeople. She has chosen elements to fit almost any design project, from starkly linear or angular forms to highly convoluted fantasies in ribbon, incorporating curved, rounded, horizontal, vertical and oblique devices. Some are plain; others are embroidered, edged with filigree, or adorned with tassels and streamers. Some are tiny; others fill a whole page.

While many of the design elements are purely decorative, there is an abundance of figurative imagery: florals, single and in sprays, garlands, wreaths and bouquets; animals real and mythical; cherubs, angels, nymphs, nudes, heralds, knights and jesters; trade cuts emblematic of printing, shipping, agriculture, medicine and music; patriotic motifs (a full display of beribboned American flags and eagles appears on pages 52–57); landscape vignettes—all festooned, encircled or entwined with scrollwork.

Copyright-free and ready for reproduction, the graphics in this book have virtually unlimited possibilities for use. The ease with which type can be set in unusual curves by modern photocomposition opens new options for filling the spaces. Anyone who delights in the creation of ruffles and drapery will find endless inspiration in this volume.

Copyright © 1983 by Dover Publications, Inc.
All rights reserved under Pan American and International Copyright Conventions.

Published in Canada by General Publishing Company, Ltd., 30 Lesmill Road, Don Mills, Toronto, Ontario.

Banners, Ribbons & Scrolls: An Archive for Artists and Designers/503 Copyright-Free Designs is a new work, first published by Dover Publications, Inc., in 1983.
The selection and arrangement of the graphics are by Carol Belanger Grafton. The research and Publisher's Note are by Joseph M. Cahn.

DOVER *Pictorial Archive* SERIES

Manufactured in the United States of America
Dover Publications, Inc., 31 East 2nd Street, Mineola, N.Y. 11501

Library of Congress Cataloging in Publication Data

Main entry under title:

Banners, ribbons, and scrolls.

(Dover pictorial archive series)
1. Flags. 2. Ribbons. 3. Scrolls. 4. Decoration and ornament. I. Grafton, Carol Belanger. II. Series.
NK1580.B3 1983   745.4   82-17818
ISBN 0-486-24443-1

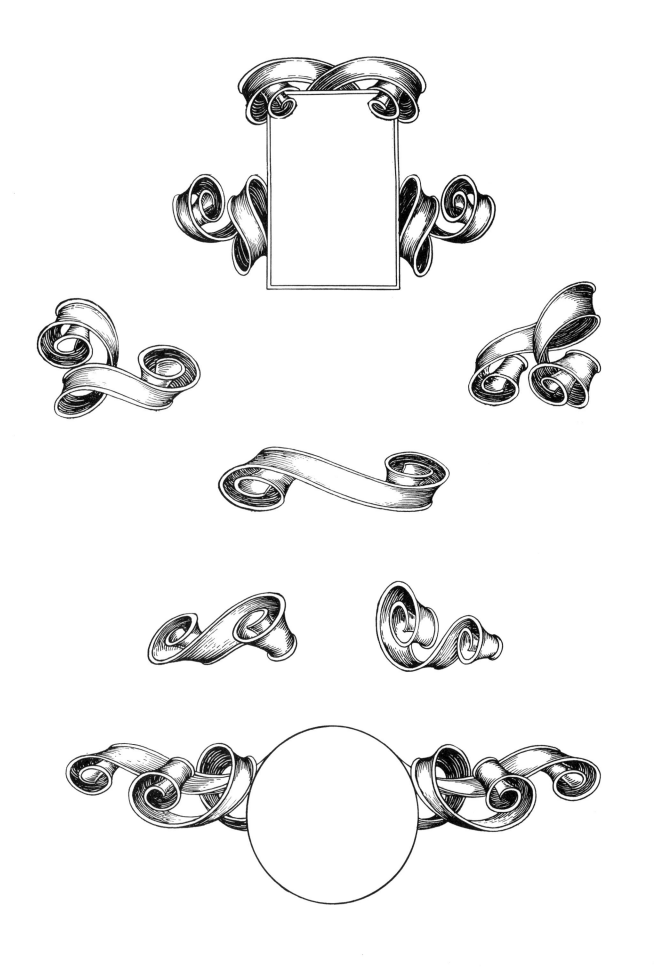

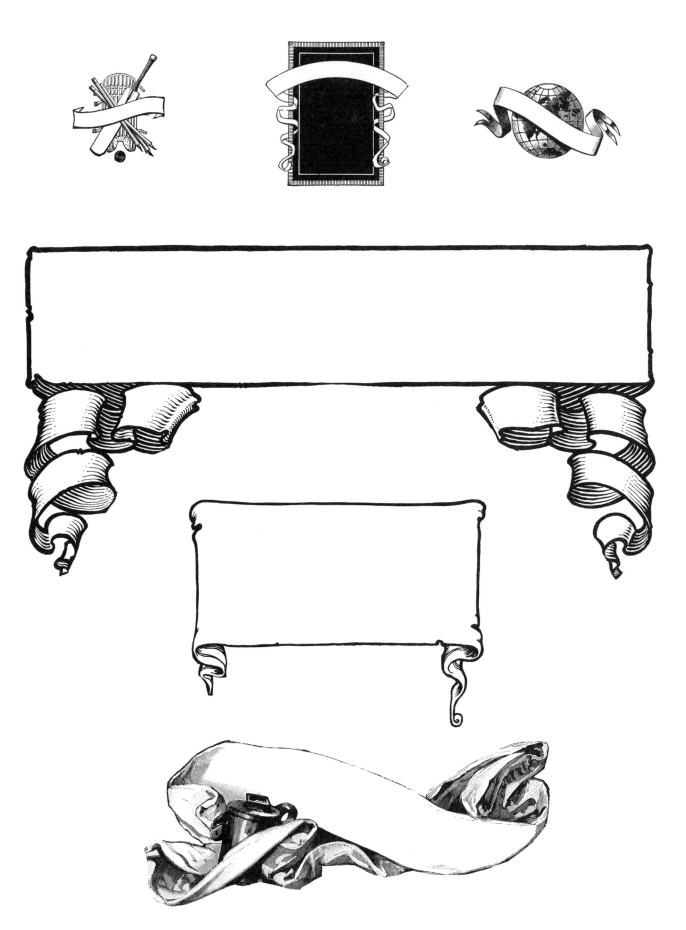

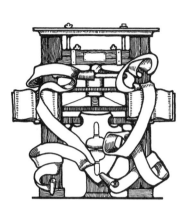

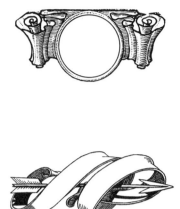

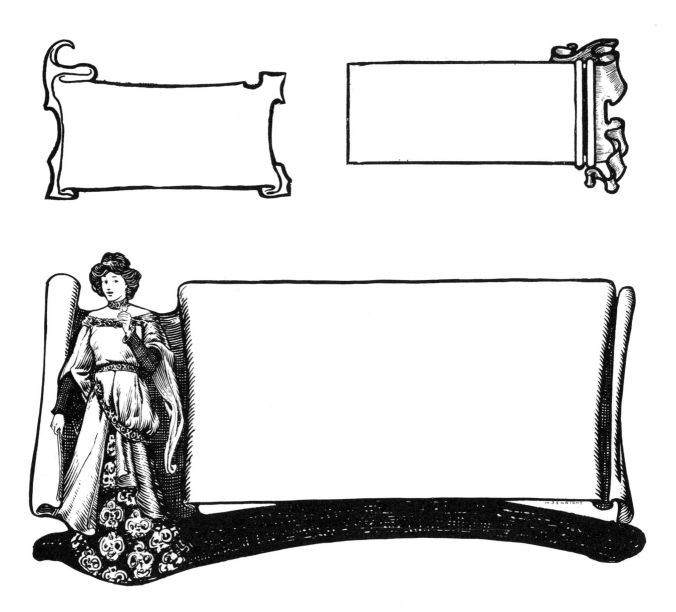

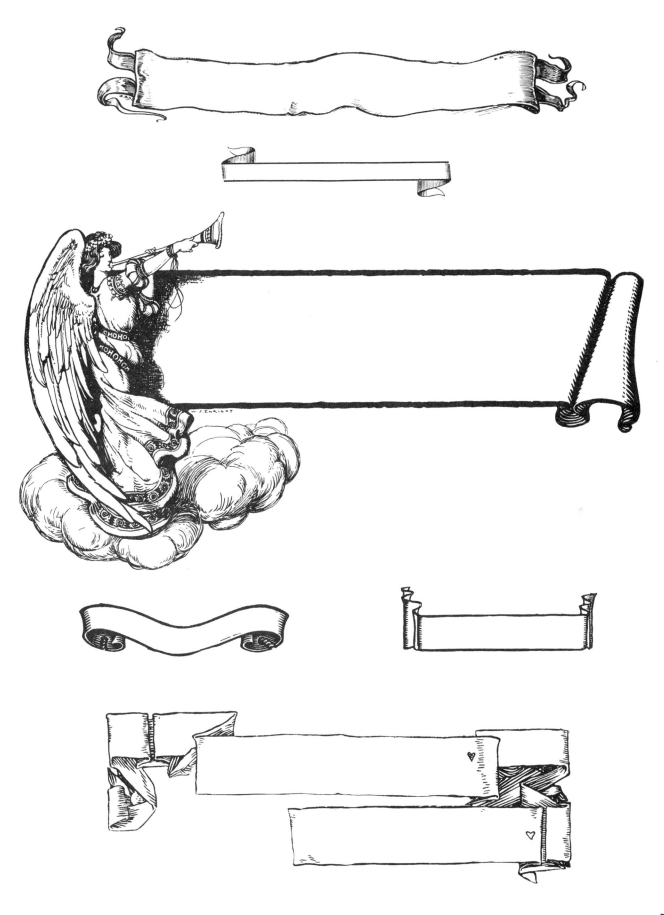

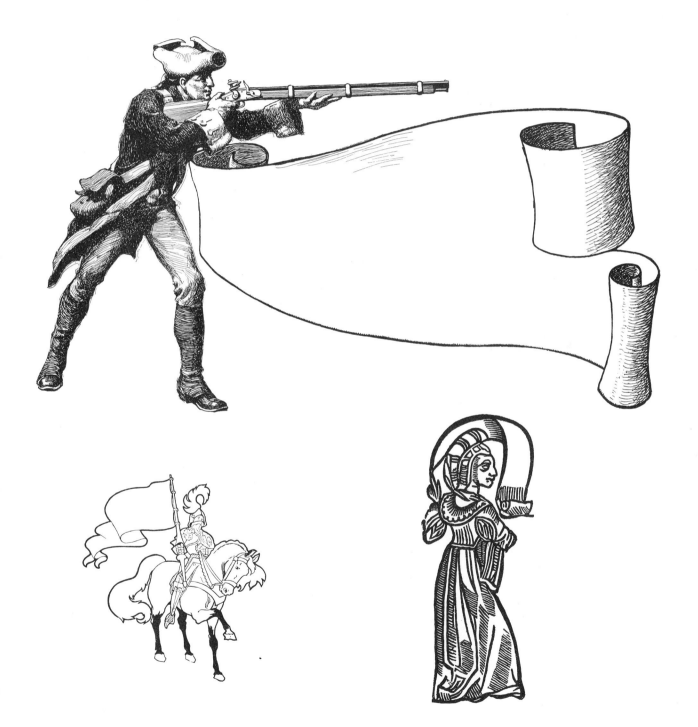

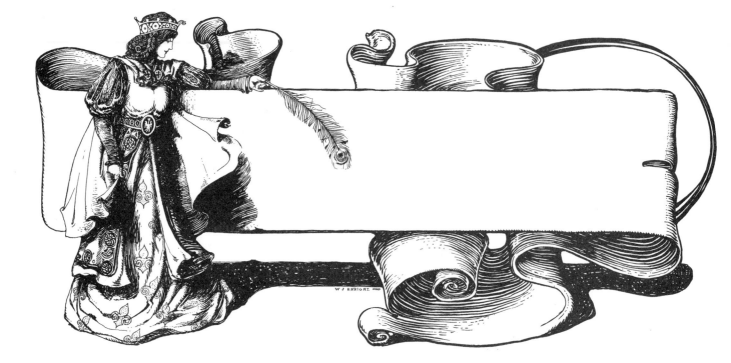

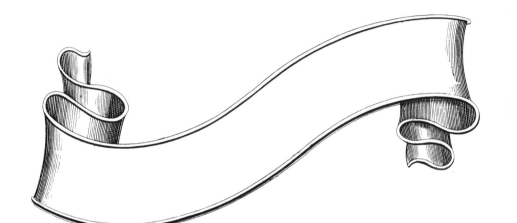

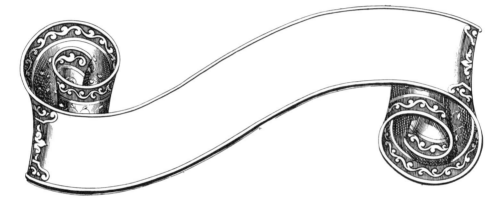

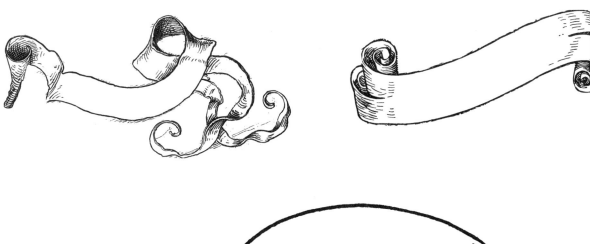

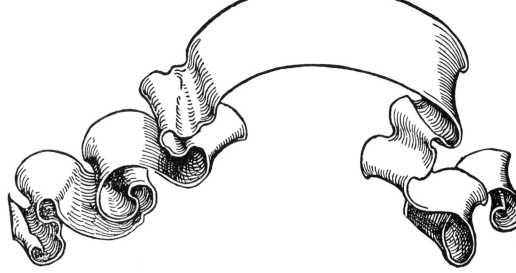

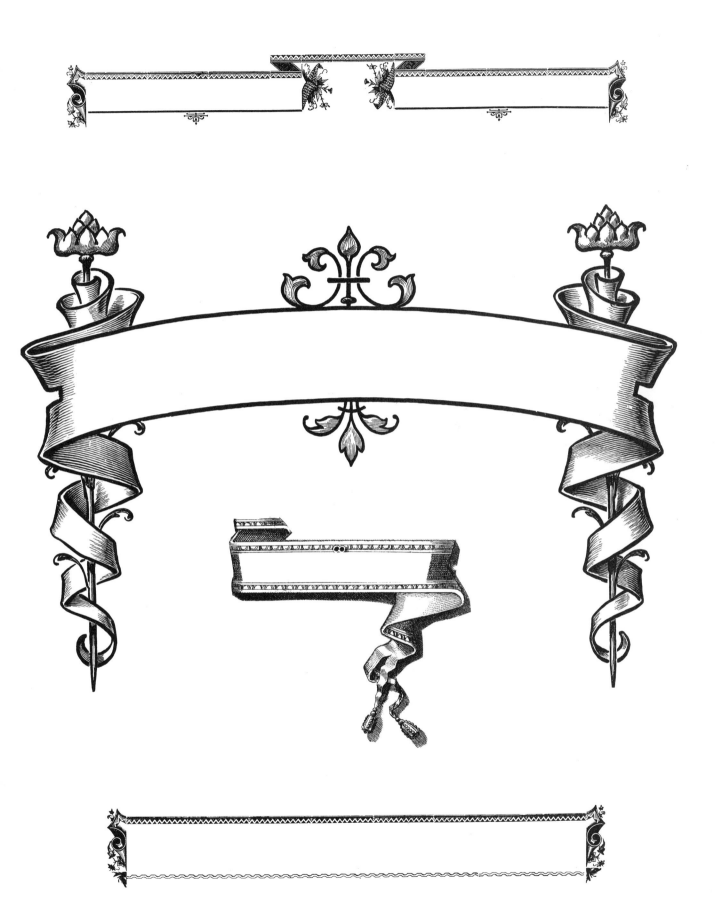

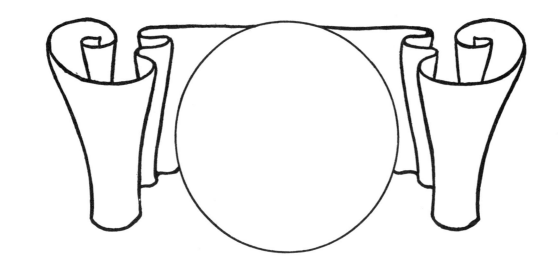

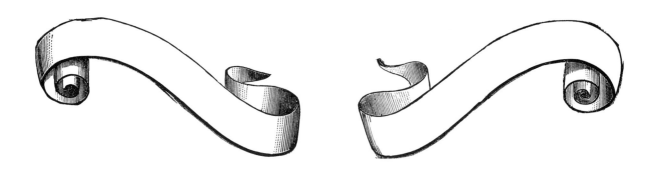

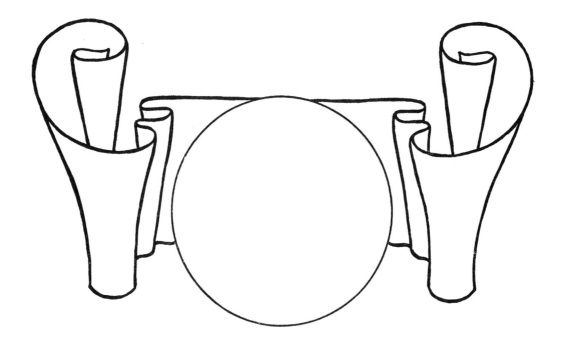

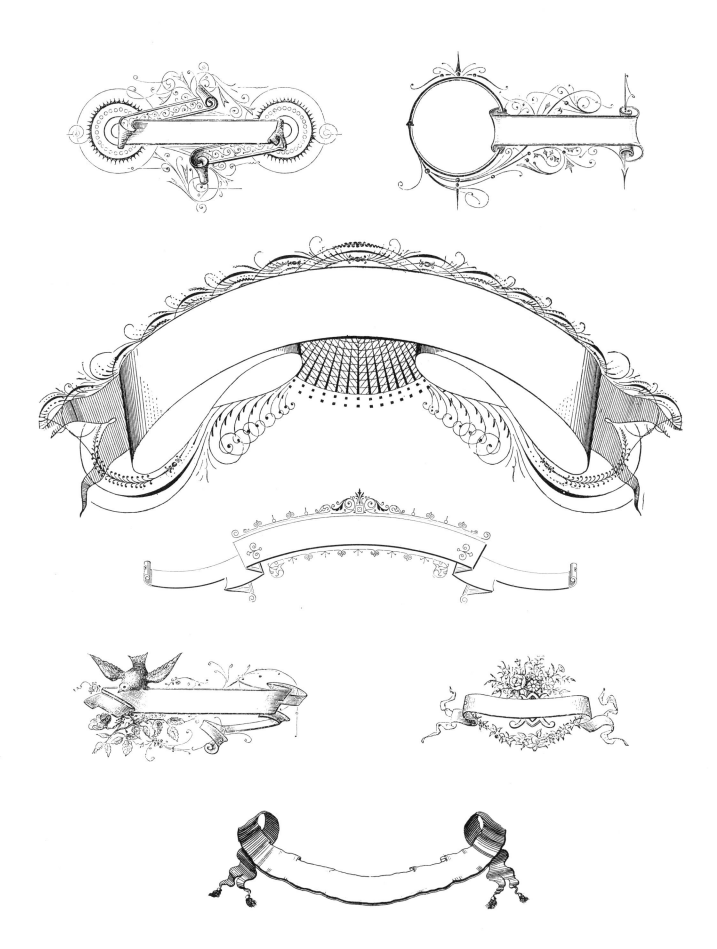

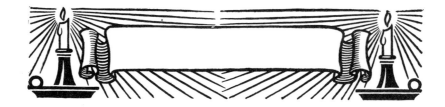

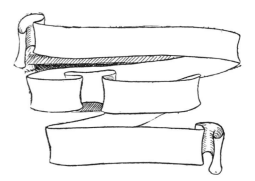

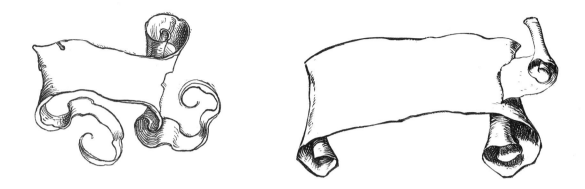

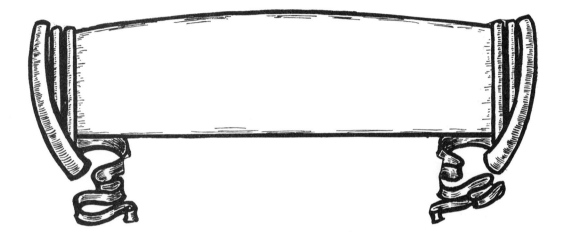

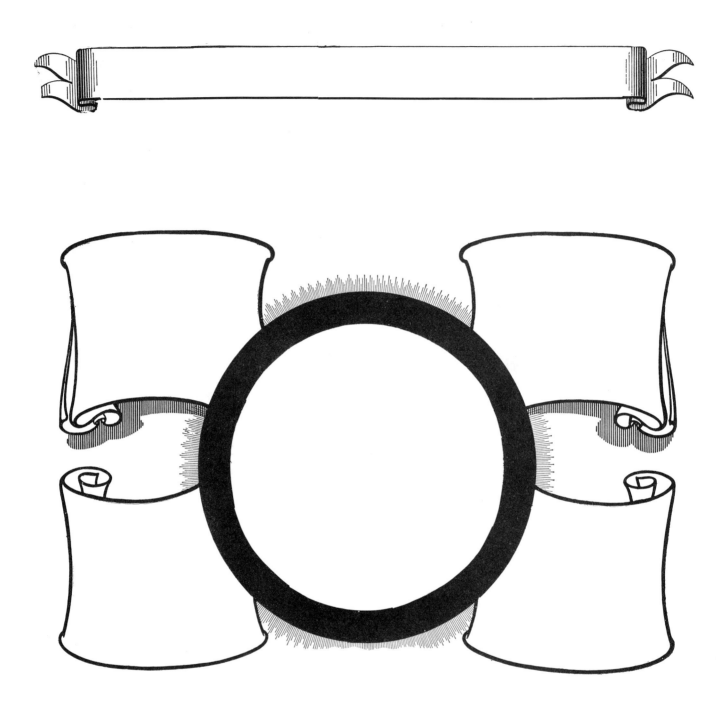

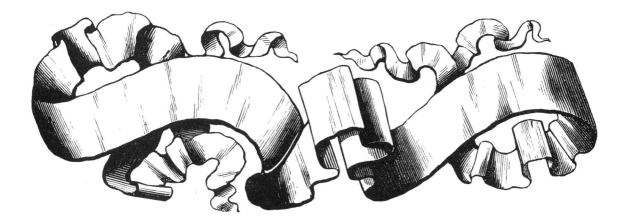

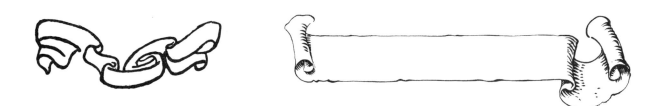

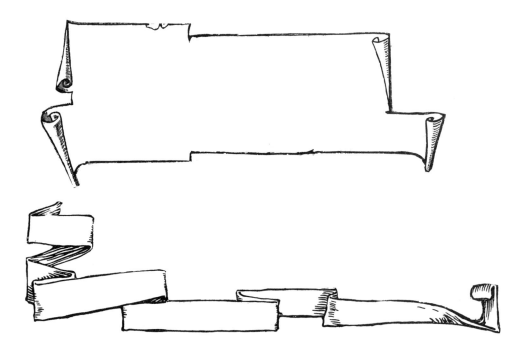

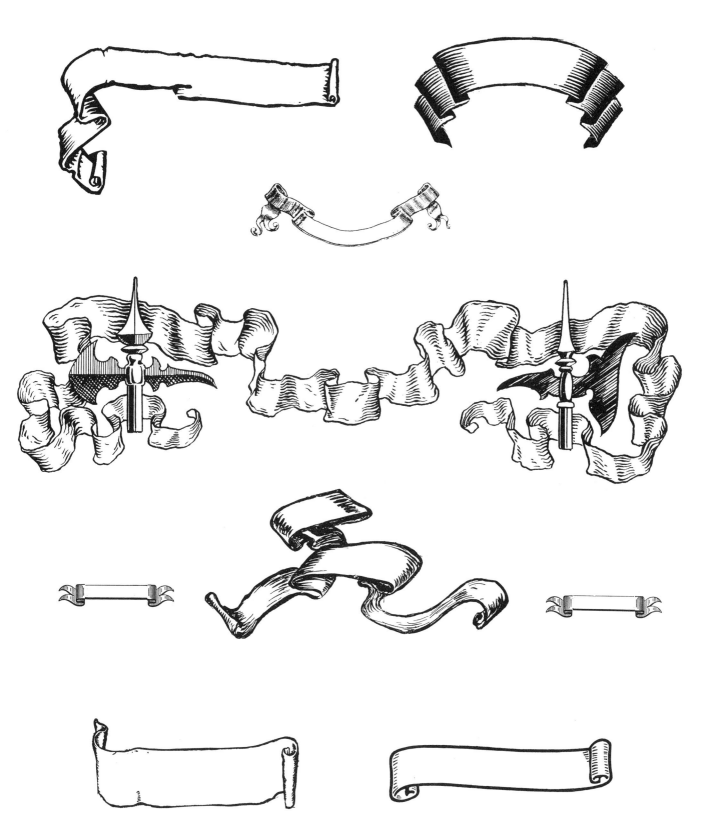

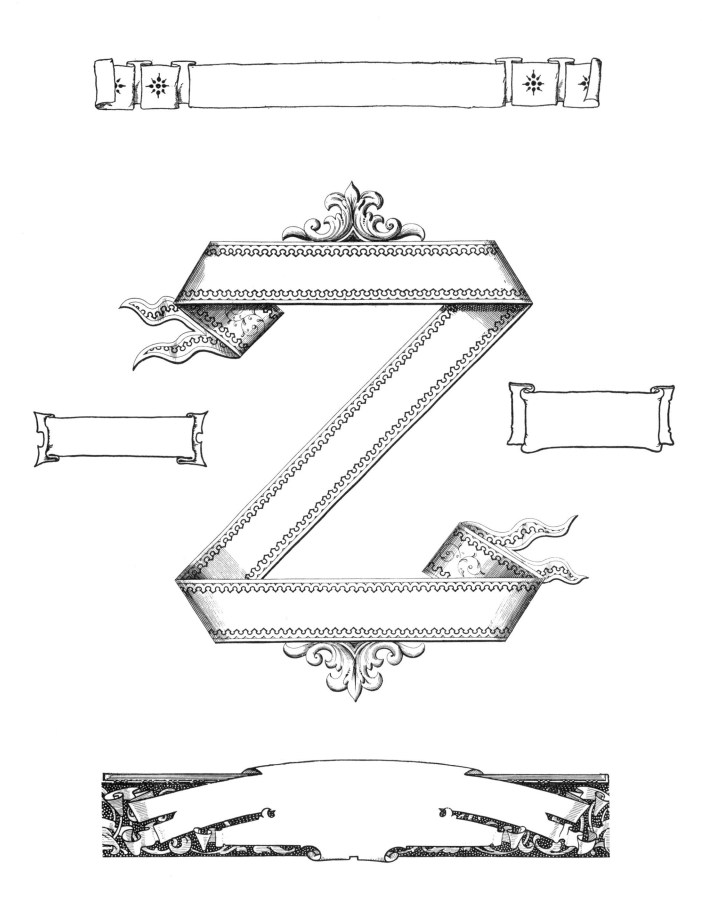

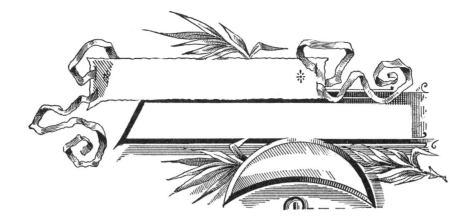

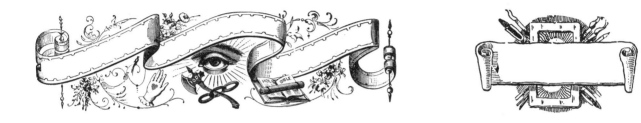

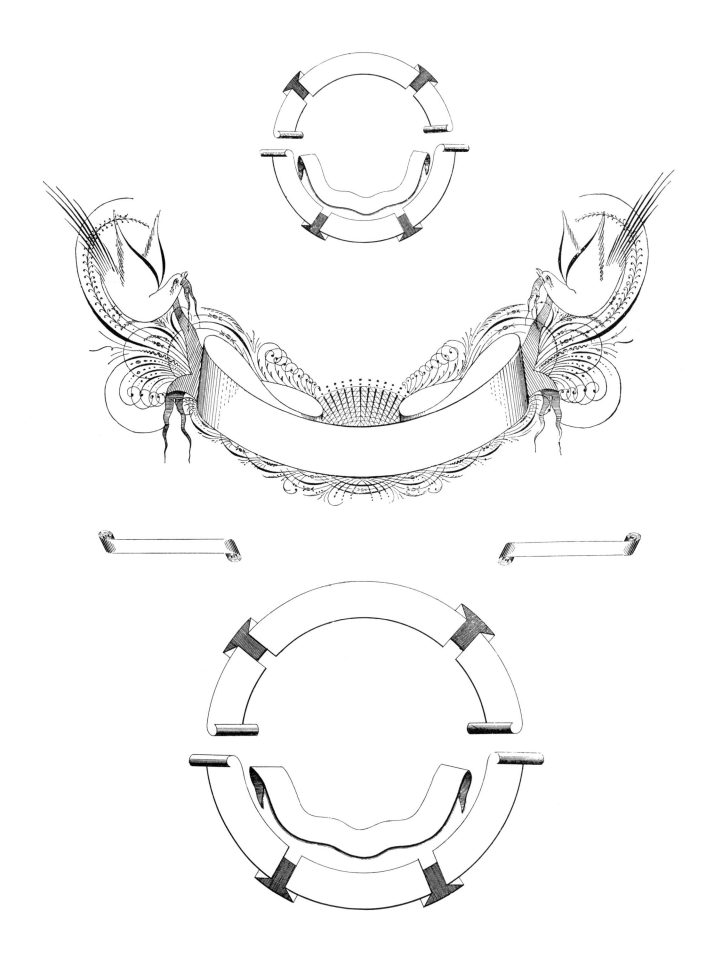

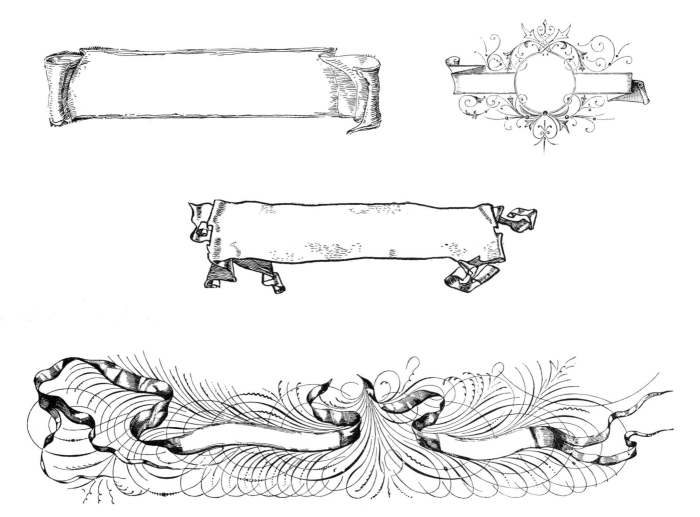

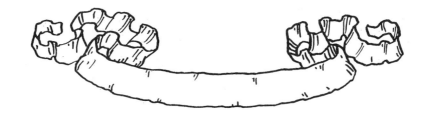

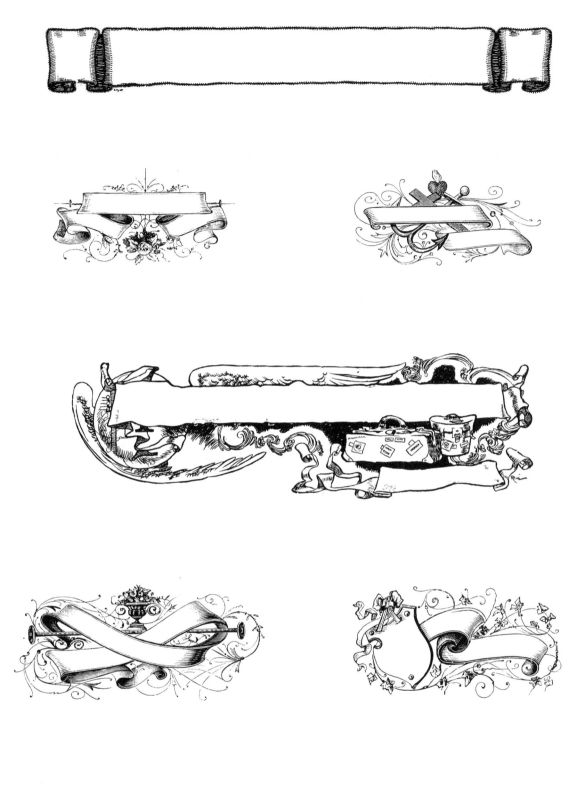

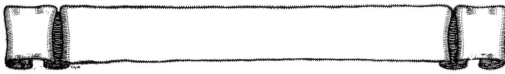

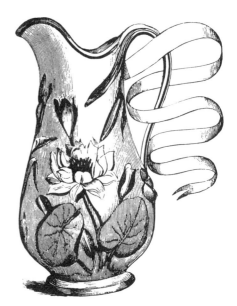

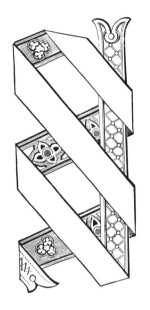

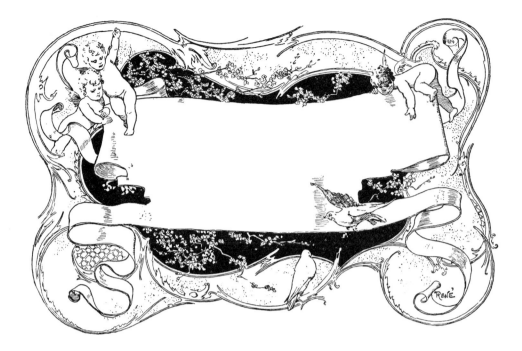

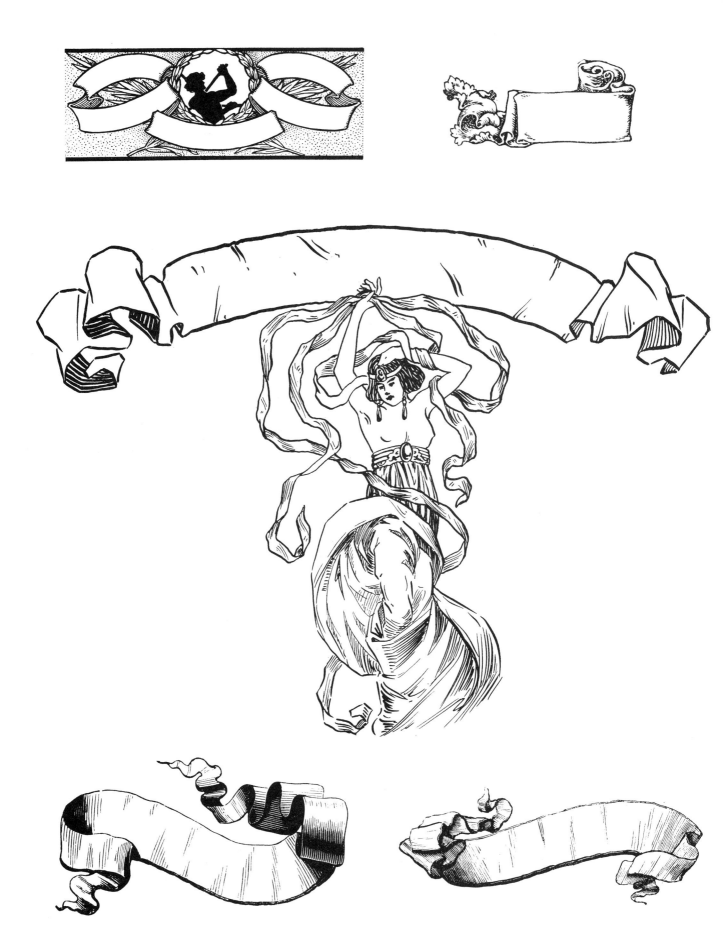

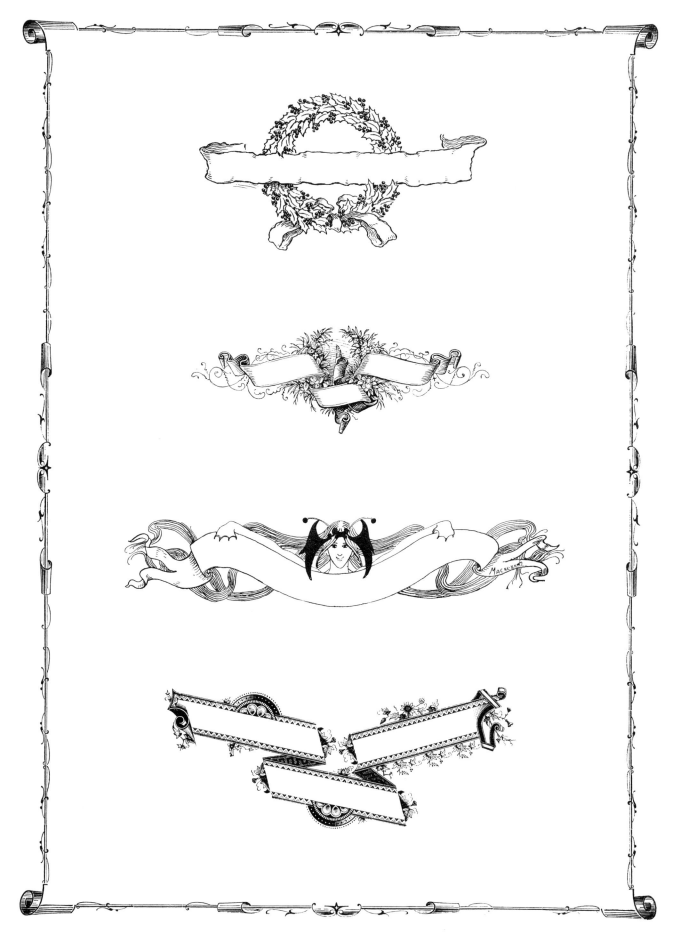

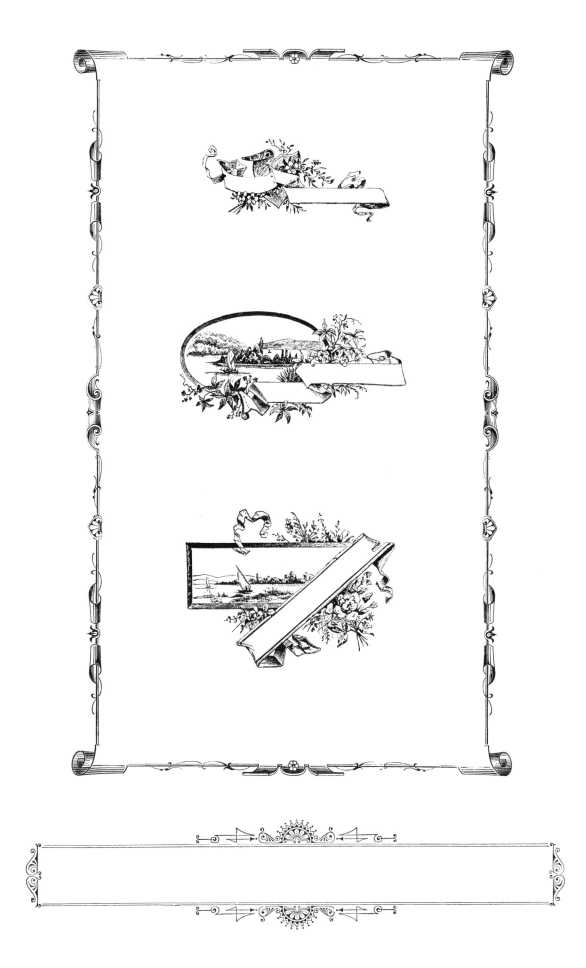

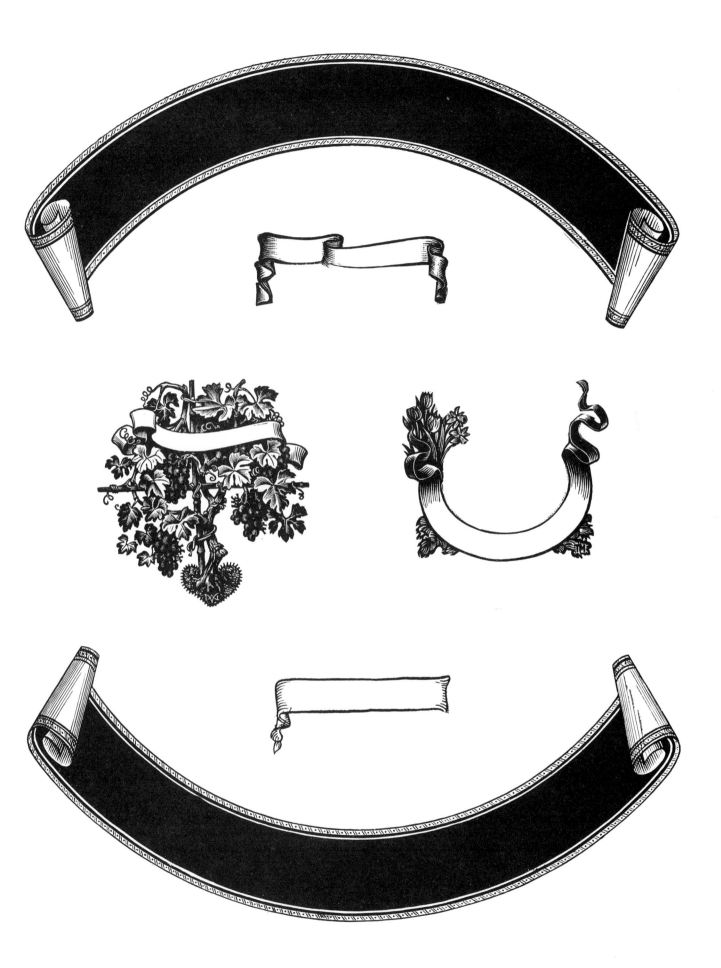

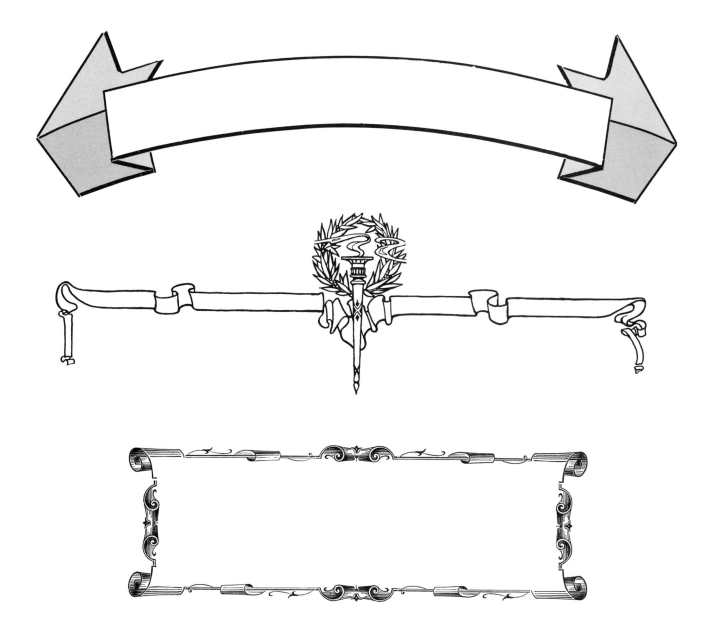

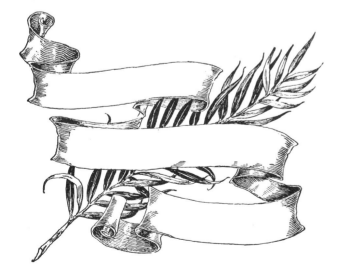

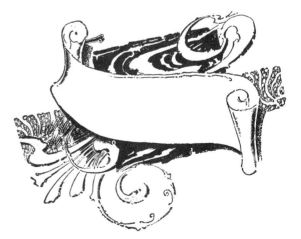

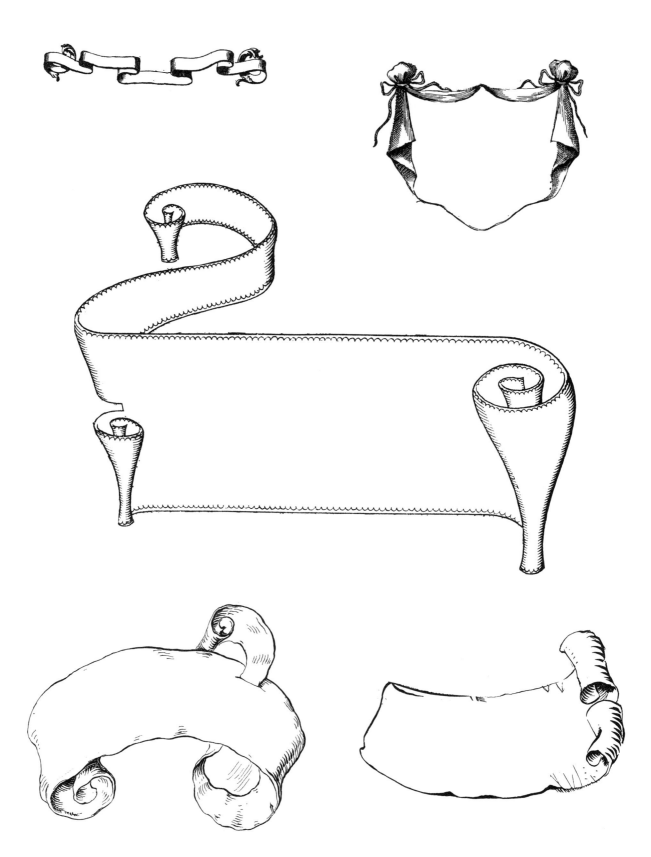

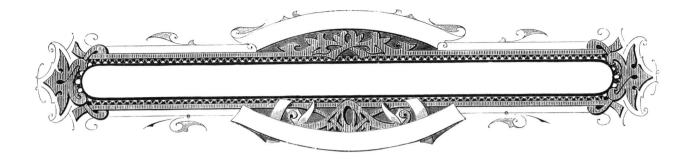

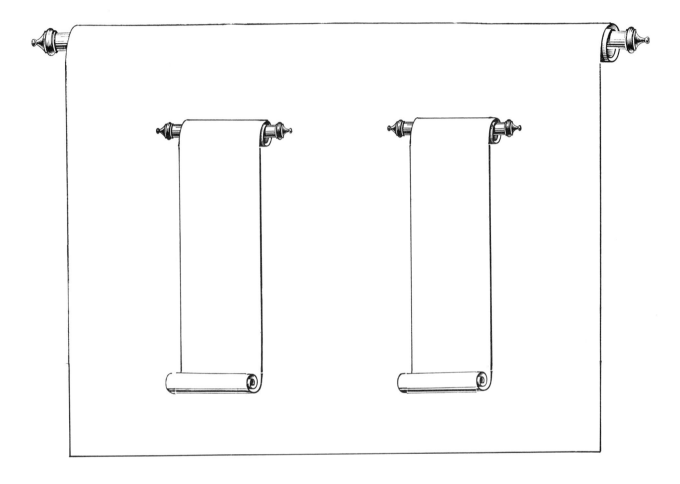

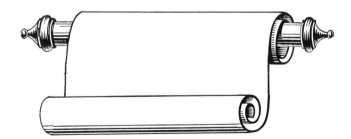

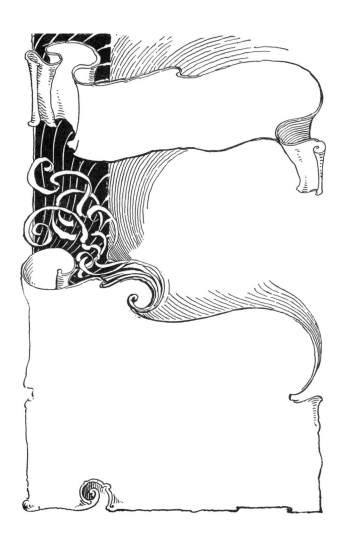

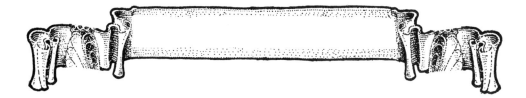

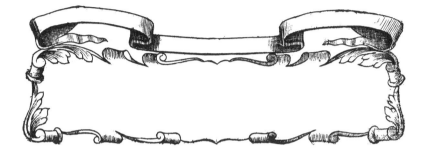

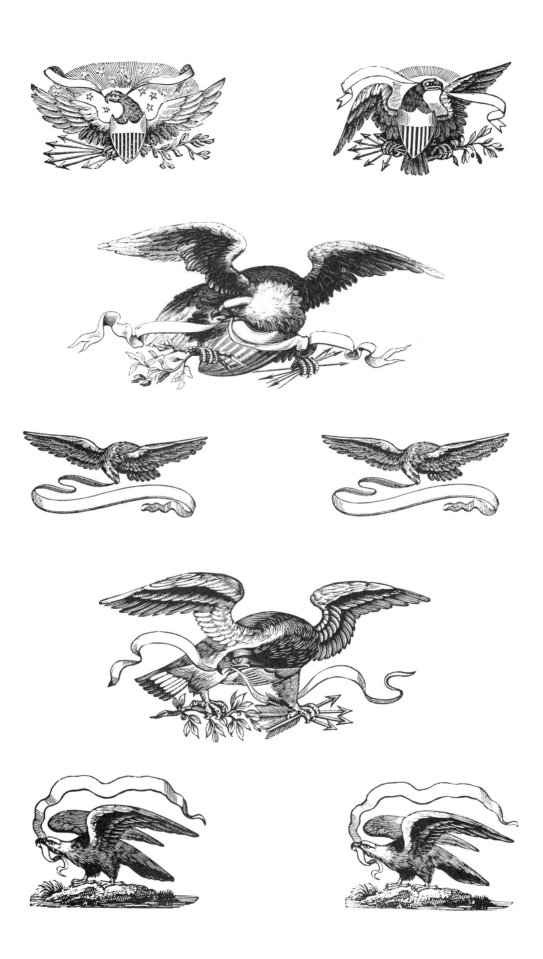

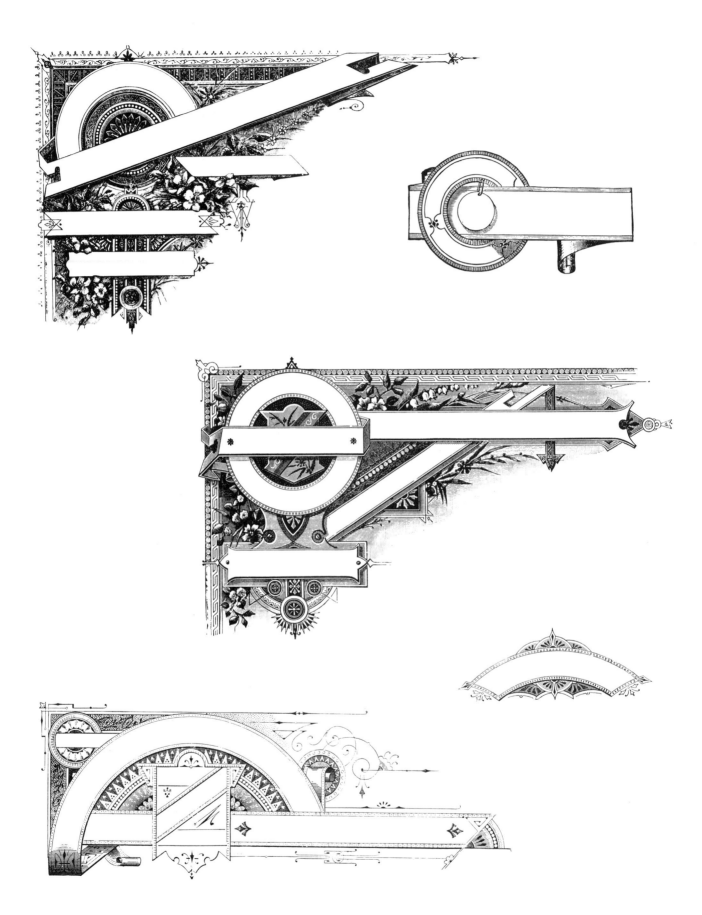

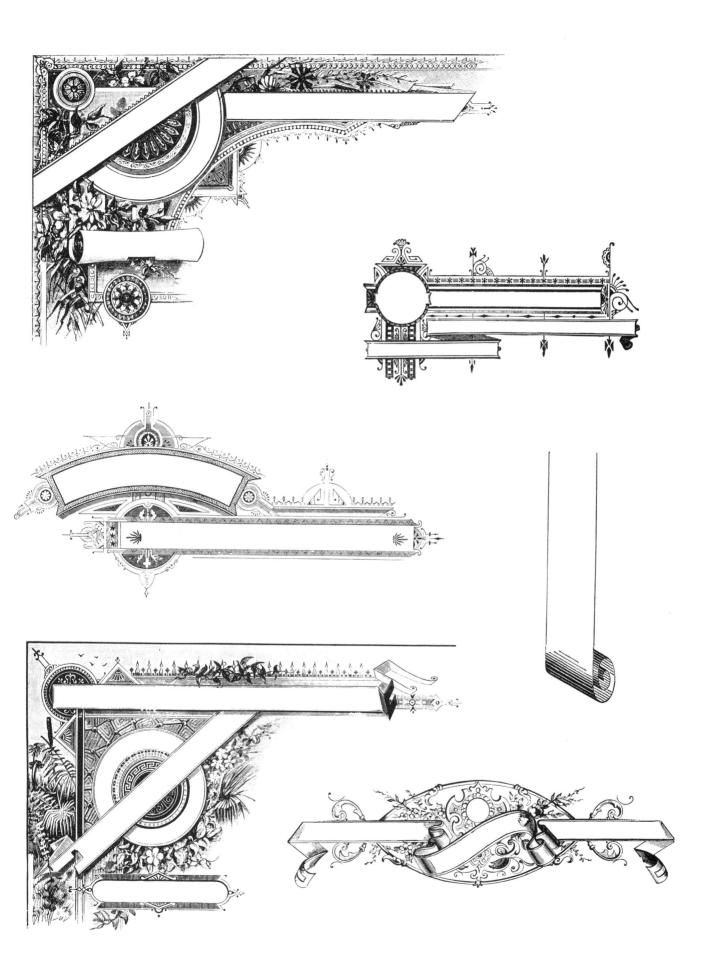

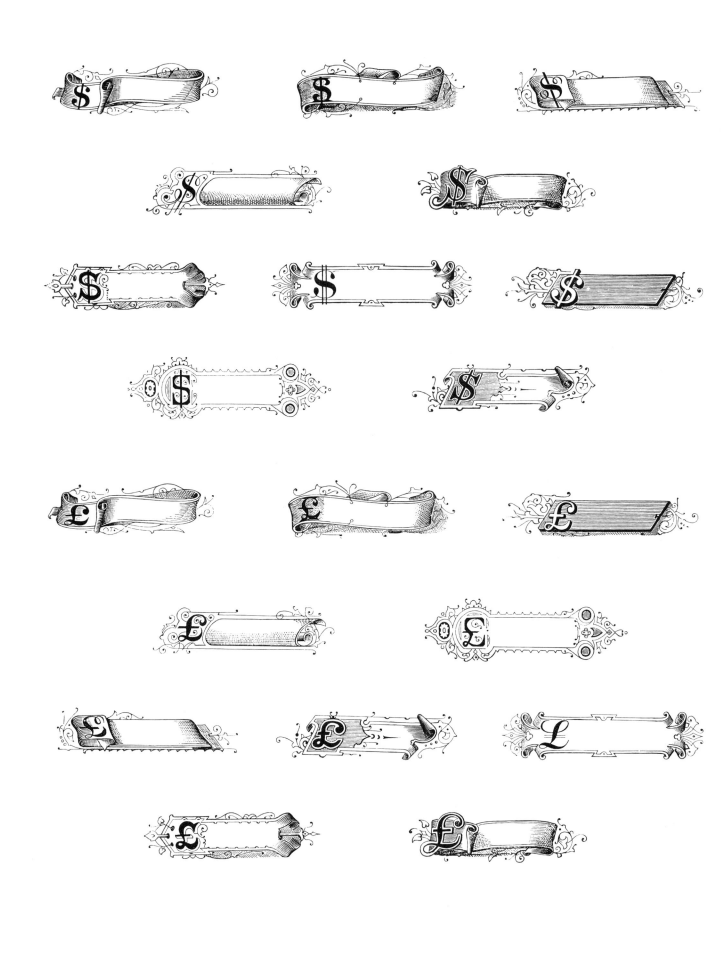

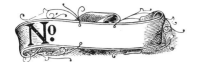

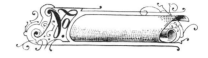

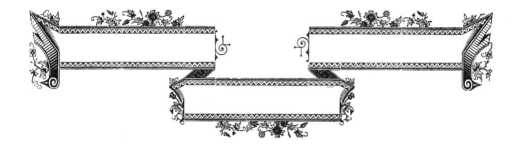

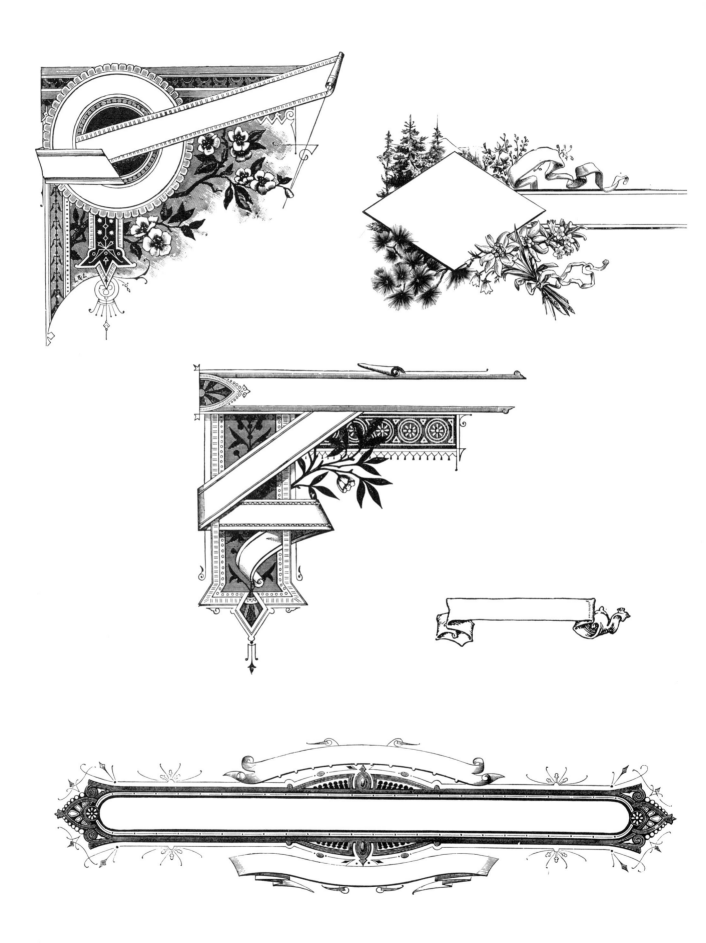

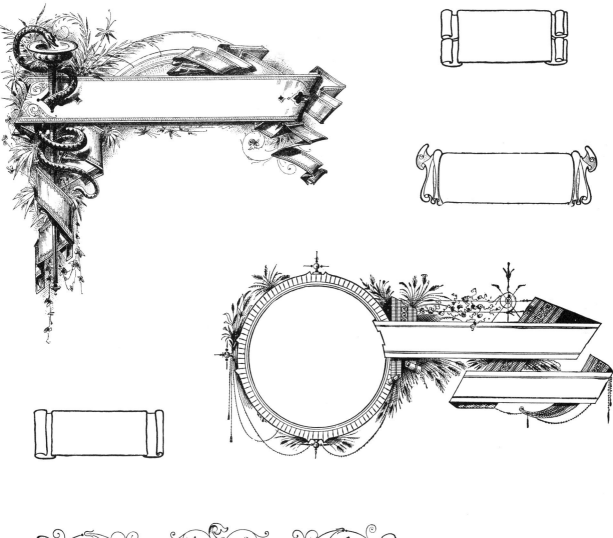

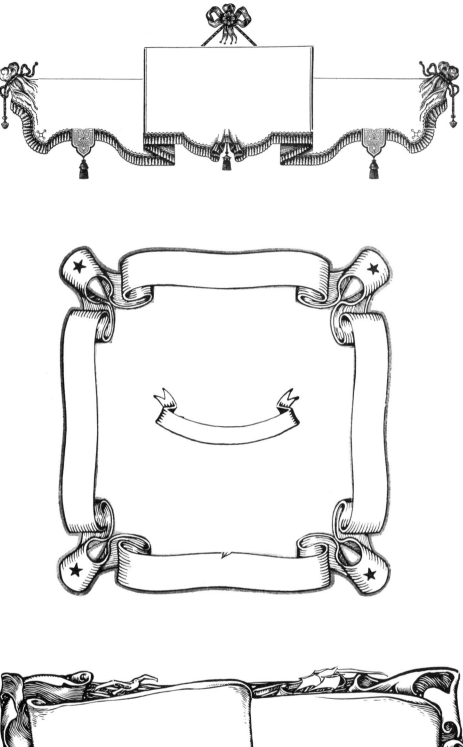

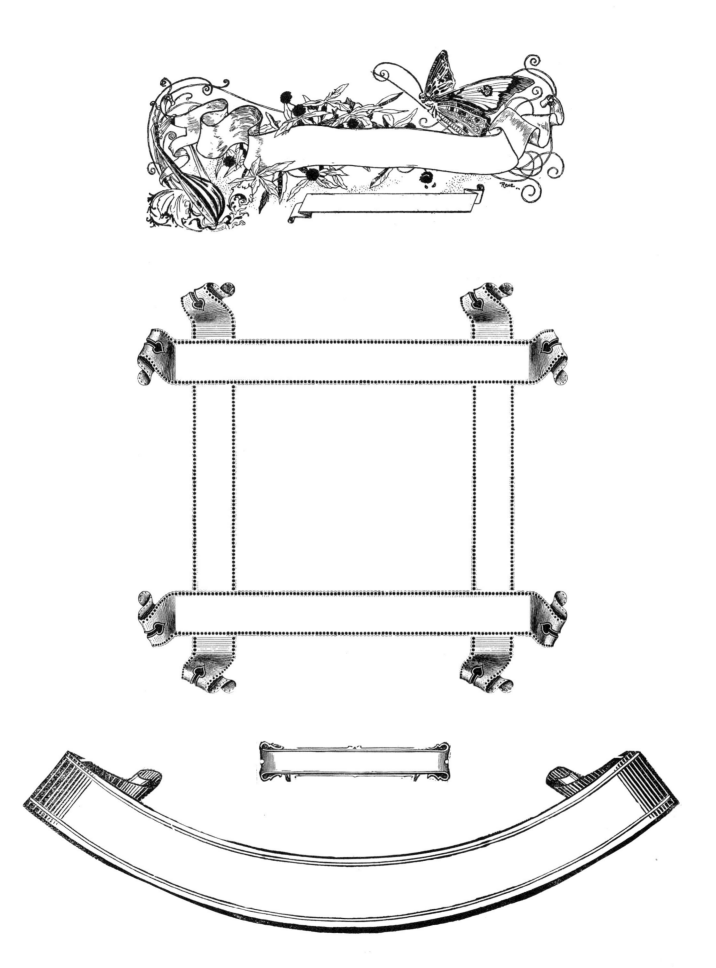

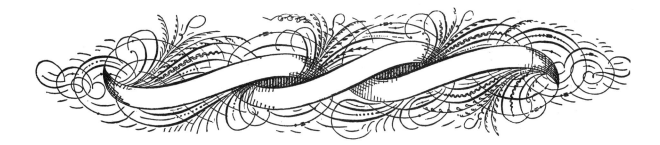

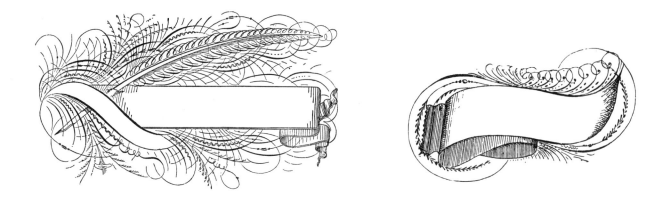

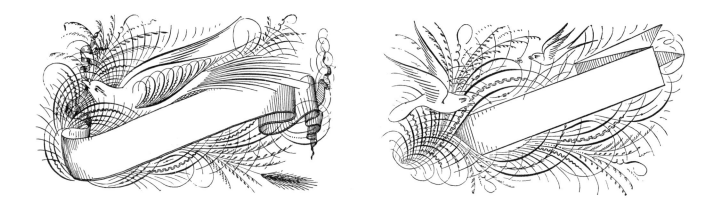

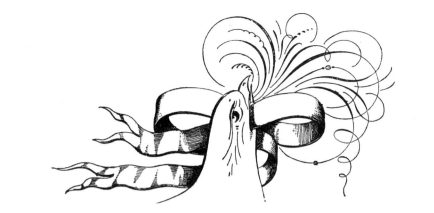

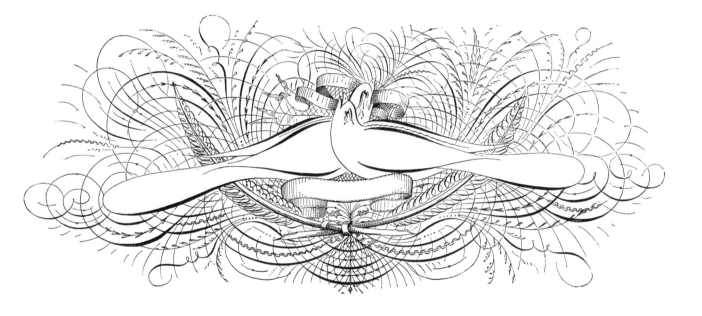

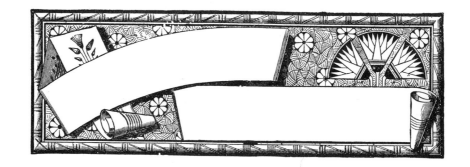

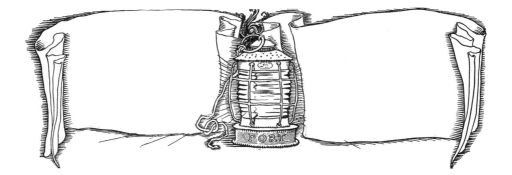

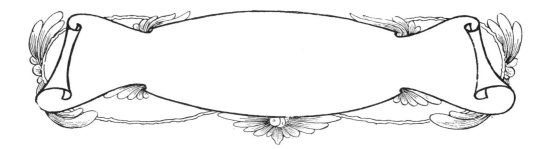

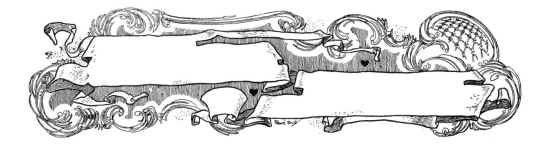

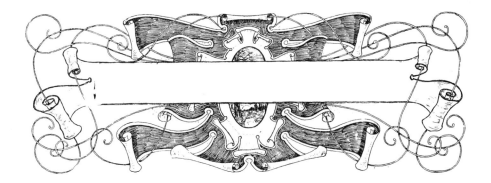

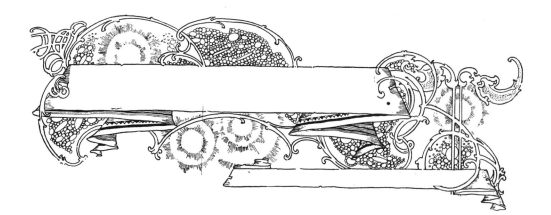

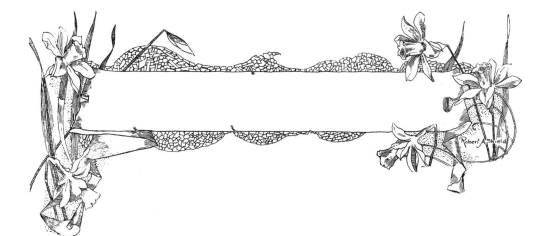

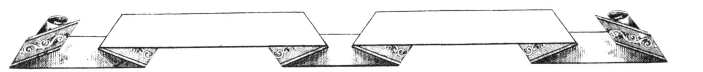

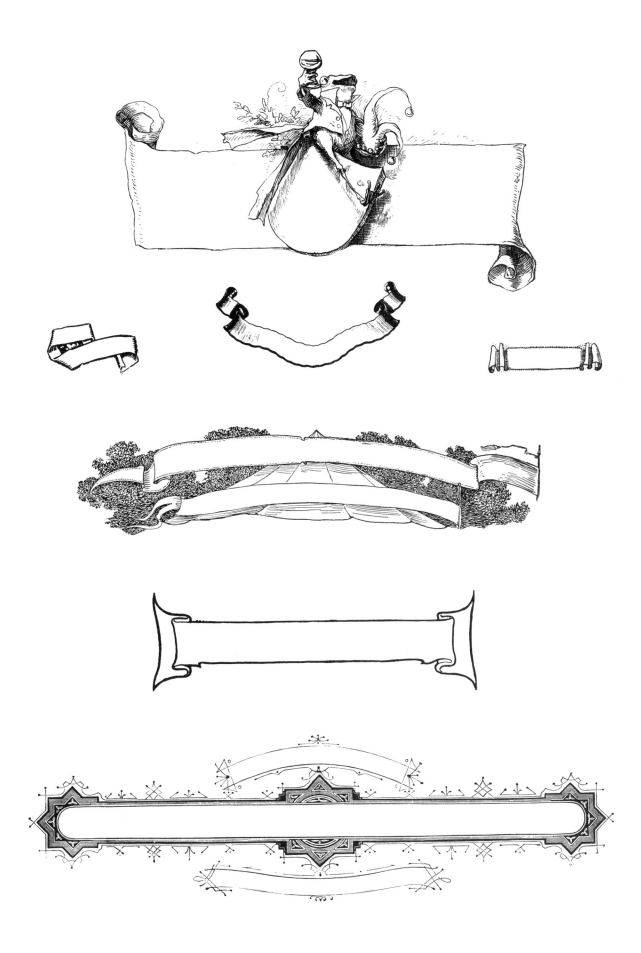

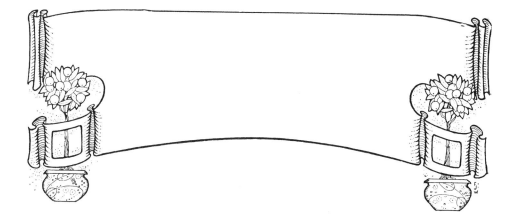

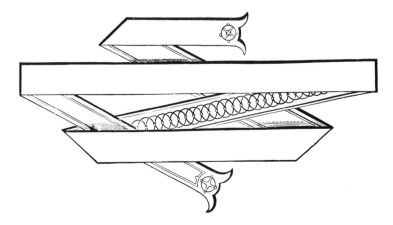

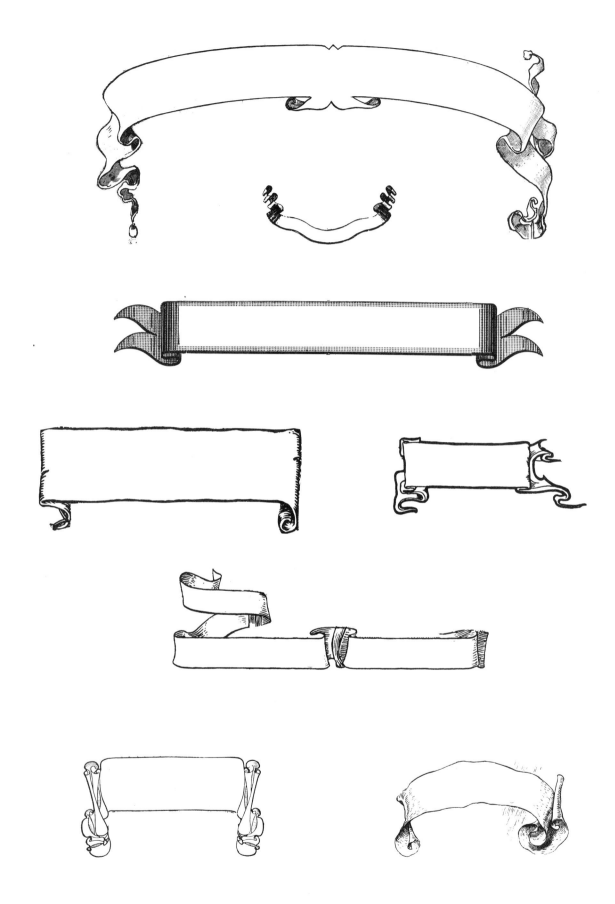

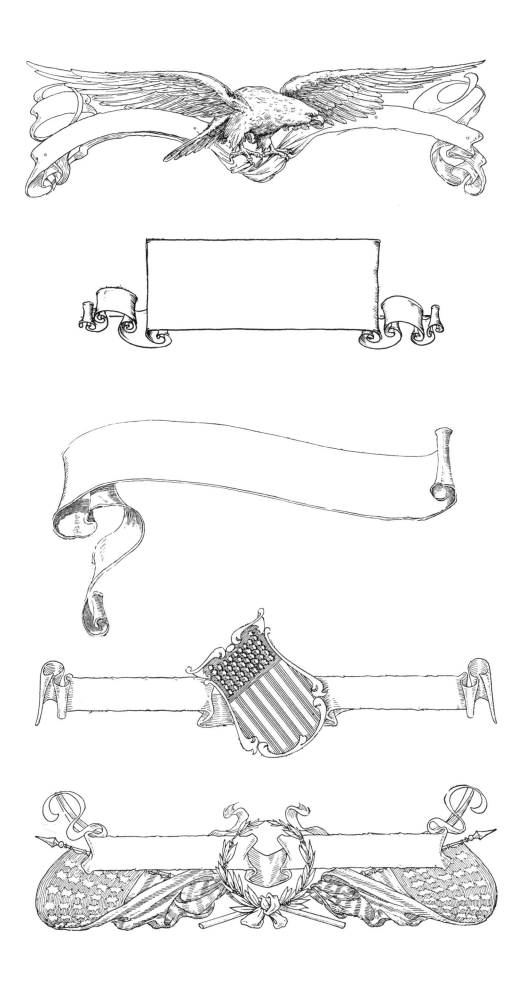

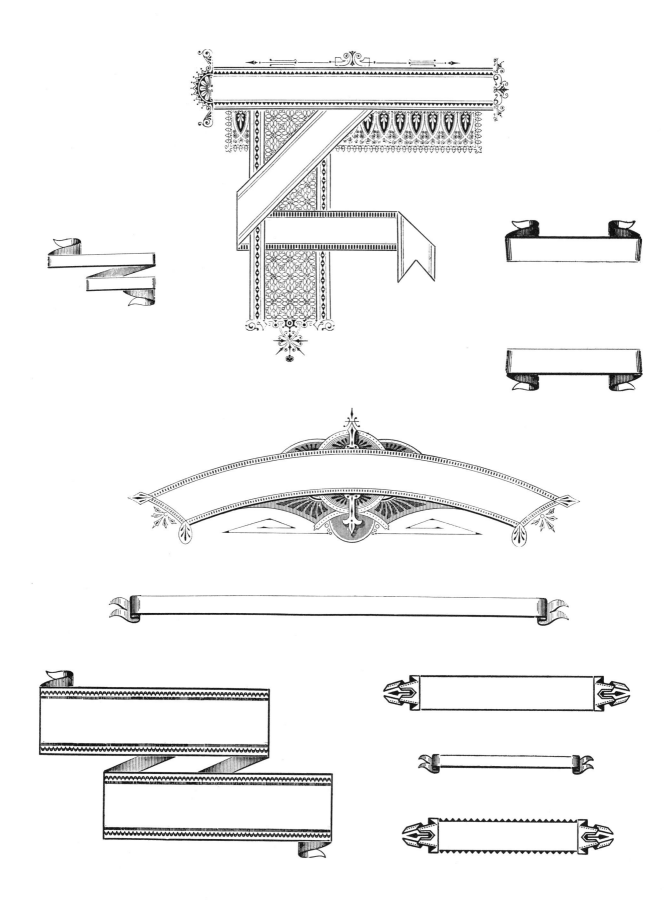

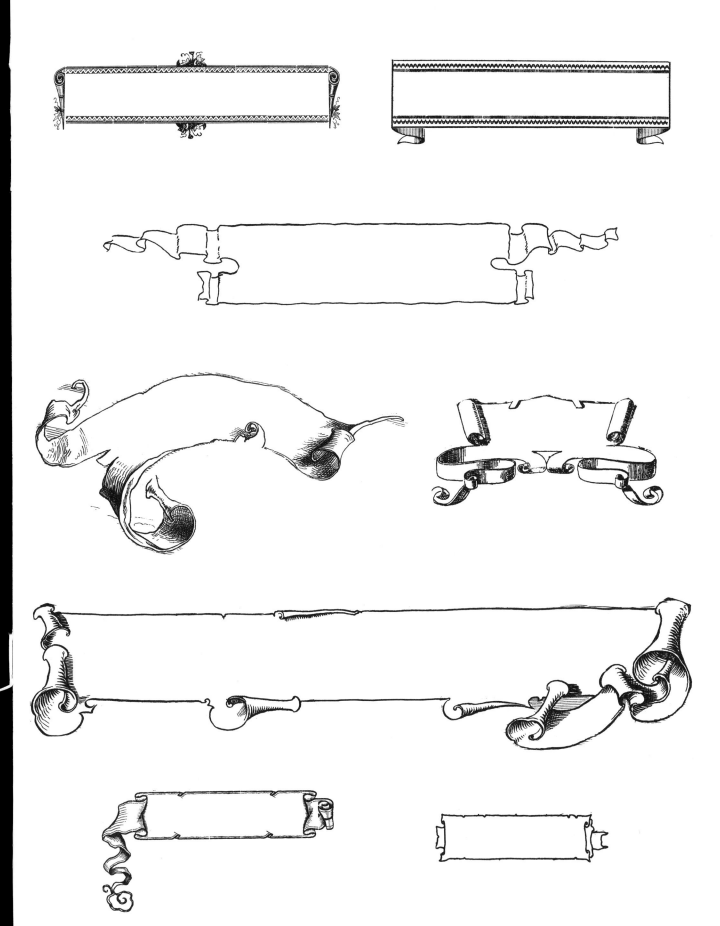

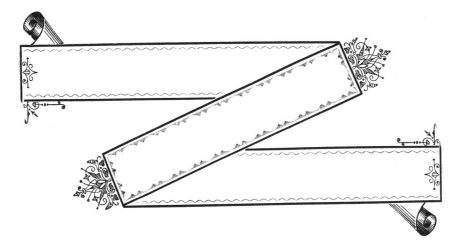

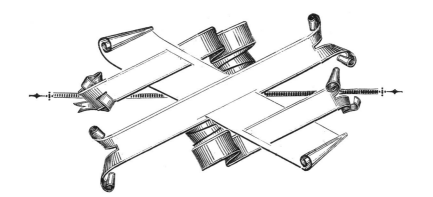

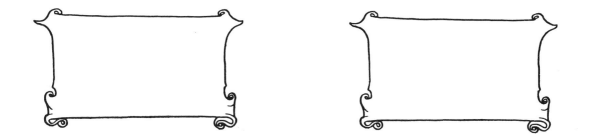

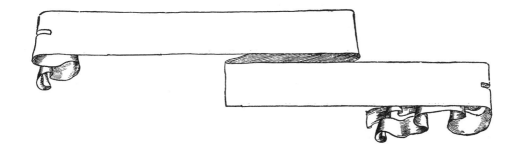

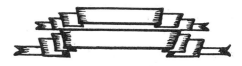

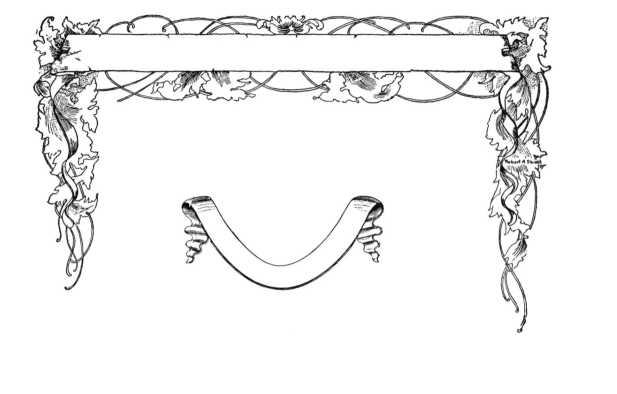

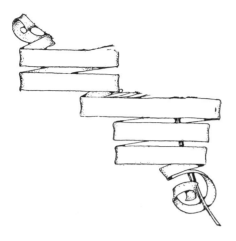
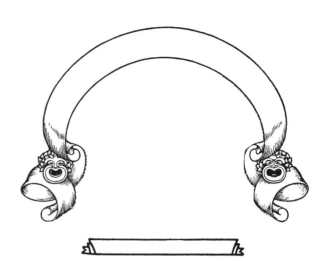
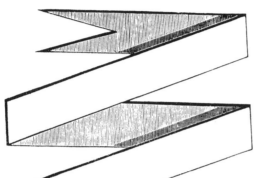
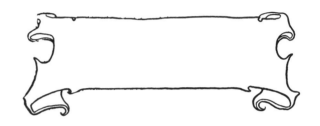

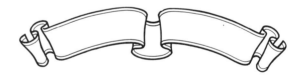

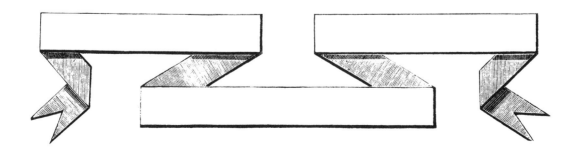

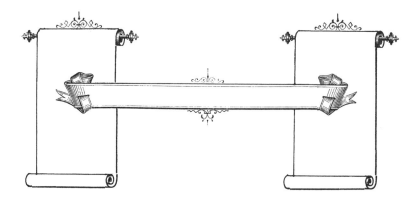

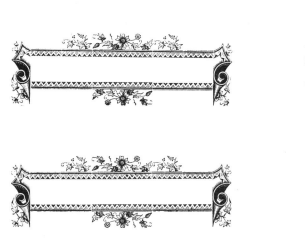

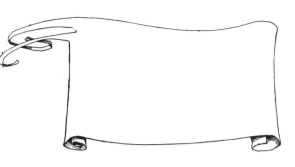

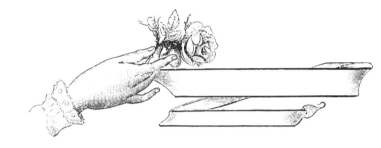

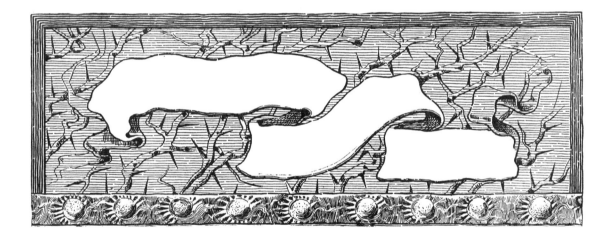

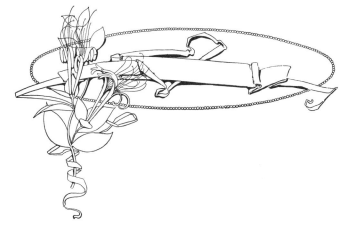